MY JOURNEY STARTS HERE

GENEVIEVE MORA

JAZZ THORNTON

MY JOURNEY STARTS HERE

A GUIDED JOURNAL TO IMPROVE YOUR MENTAL WELL-BEING

ILLUSTRATED BY FRIDA LINDSTRÖM

PENGUIN BOOKS

This book is dedicated to two of the
people who taught us how to fight.

Thank you Esther and Hilary for guiding us through
our individual journeys and for equipping us with the tools
to go on and help others fight through their own battles.

This book belongs to:

Name: _____

DEAR READER,

YOU HAVE PICKED UP THIS BOOK FOR A REASON. PERHAPS YOU ARE STRUGGLING — YOU ARE NOT SURE HOW TO BEGIN YOUR JOURNEY OR YOU FEEL AS IF YOU HAVE BEEN TREADING WATER. WHATEVER THE REASON MAY BE, THANK YOU FOR TAKING THE BRAVE STEP TO START YOUR JOURNEY TO WELLNESS.

AS TWO WOMEN WHO HAVE FOUGHT MENTAL ILLNESS AND GONE THROUGH MANY LIFE STRUGGLES, WE KNOW HOW CHALLENGING AND EXHAUSTING IT IS. WE ALSO KNOW THAT WITH THE RIGHT TOOLS, SUPPORT AND HOPE, YOU CAN GET THROUGH IT.

WE ARE PROOF.

YOU ARE WORTHY OF RECOVERY AND DESERVING OF SUPPORT. THERE IS NO BETTER TIME TO START YOUR JOURNEY THAN NOW. YOU ARE STRONG ENOUGH TO FIGHT THIS.

WE BELIEVE IN YOU.

YOUR JOURNEY STARTS HERE...

Jazz x *Genevieve*

CONTENTS

MOVE ✖✖✖✖✖

IT'S NOT ABOUT BATTLING YOUR PAST, BUT FIGHTING FOR YOUR FUTURE.

— JAZZ THORNTON

Hey there!

Thank you so much for choosing to pick up this journal. My name is Jazz Thornton. Some of you may know me as the author of *Stop Surviving Start Fighting* or the director of the show *Jessica's Tree* or just as a mental health advocate. For those of you who don't know me, however, let me tell you a little about myself.

I grew up in a small town in New Zealand. Following trauma starting when I was 3 years old, and severe bullying growing up, I entered a long and hard battle with mental illness, with my first attempt to take my life at 12 years old. I spent the next 9 years in and out of hospitals and mental health wards fighting my own mind. It felt like it was a fight that would never be won — but I did it. I beat it. This journal is filled with practical tools that both Gen and I used to help us recover. To fight and gain our lives back. I hope that this journal helps you, inspires you and gives you the fighting tools to take on the world.

Hope is real, change is possible.

Heya, my name is Genevieve!

(also known as G, Gen or Giraffe)

I spent the majority of my teenage years fighting anxiety, OCD and anorexia. I thought my life was going to be that way forever but with incredible support, love and tools I managed to get to where I am today, the proud co-founder of Voices of Hope.

If you've picked up this book I imagine you are going through your own struggles, so let me remind you that you are stronger than you think. Yes, it can be overwhelming, exhausting, and seem never-ending but if anything I hope my story reminds you that no matter what you are going through, you can get through.

I am excited for you and hope this book gives you the strength to keep on going.

Sending you lots of love,

Genevieve

WELCOME TO

MY JOURNEY STARTS HERE.

A GUIDED JOURNAL TO IMPROVE YOUR MENTAL WELL-BEING

We have separated this journey into 3 different sections called 'phases of the battle'.

Prepare, Act and Move are the areas we have chosen to help guide you through this journal and your fight to wellness. While every person and their experience is different, it is our hope that this journal equips you with tools to learn how to fight through various situations, mindsets and destructive thought patterns. There is no right way to use this journal. This is for YOU! However, we do suggest starting at the beginning and making your way through. As new things arise, you can always go back to previous pages and add your new thoughts and ideas in too.

Do everything in your own time and remember, healing isn't linear.

You have made the very first step by choosing to pick up this journal and begin your journey.

MY YEAR IN COLOUR

Visualising your emotions so you can track them on a daily basis can be a really helpful tool in your journey. Tracking your mood in colours on a scale of 1–5 can help you notice patterns and identify the days which were good and the days which weren't so good. This can help you notice if certain things contribute to the not so good days and to the good days!

Looking at these patterns can help you, as a motivation to make more of your days a positive colour. Make yesterday's lows a reason to turn your today into a happier colour.

Fill out these circles below using 5 different colours and then refer to the chart on the next page daily to track your overall mood.

Remember that ups and downs are a normal part of life and no one lives with a 5 star mood all the time!

THERE IS NO NEED TO WAIT FOR A 'NEW YEAR, NEW ME' TO START CHANGING YOUR HABITS OR BEHAVIOURS.

	J	F	M	A	M	J	J	A	S	O	N	D
1												
2												
3												
4												
5												
6												
7												
8												
9												
10												
11												
12												
13												
14												
15												
16												
17												
18												
19												
20												
21												
22												
23												
24												
25												
26												
27												
28												
29												
30												
31												

PREPARE

The first stage of an army battle is the preparation phase. This is where people research what they are fighting and prepare themselves for the battle. We have filled this section with tools, lists and activities to help you prepare for your fight. Some of these may seem simple, but they are proactive tools that will set you up well. They are also things that you can go back to for a 'pick me up' later.

Remember, everyone's fight is different —
But every fight requires a first step. Here is yours.

THINGS I AM GRATEFUL FOR

Taking a moment to stop and think about things you are grateful for is important. This could be your family and friends, it could be sunsets or coffee — whatever these things are, take time to write them down. Go back to this list when you need a reminder of some things worth fighting for.

-
-
-
-
-
-
-
-
-
-

WHAT THINGS MAKE YOU FEEL HAPPY TO BE ALIVE?
AND HOW CAN YOU ADD MORE OF THEM INTO YOUR LIFE?

It's not easy,
but it is simple.

— Esther Greenwood

THINGS THAT MAKE ME SMILE

Things that make you smile can be used, looked at or done when you need a bit of a boost. Maybe it is photos of puppies or sunflowers or maybe it is watching fail videos on YouTube (a personal fave of Jazz's). What are some things that make you smile?

TOP 5 FAVOURITE QUOTES

Quotes are something we both used to keep us going in recovery. They are often simple yet inspiring, challenging or encouraging. What are your 5 favourite quotes?

How would you describe yourself, in a loving way, to a stranger?

WHAT DOES 'ENOUGH' MEAN TO YOU?

Reasons
why you are ENOUGH!

We can be our own worst critics,
focusing on what is 'wrong' with us and
not all the amazing things that make us
who we are. We want you to use this space to
create a list of reasons WHY you ARE enough.
If you get stuck, ask someone to help you
out. Talking about ourselves in a positive
light can be hard but it's time we
started being kind to ourselves,
just like we would be to
a friend.

Hope is not lost, our situations can sometimes just blind us from seeing it.

TOP SONGS TO PUT ME
IN A GOOD MOOD

When I was struggling I would often put on sad music to match my mood. This often made me feel even worse, so when I decided to recover, I actively chose to put on inspirational music instead of sad music when I was feeling low. What are your top feel-good songs?

Jazz x

-
-
-
-
-
-
-
-
-
-

YOU HAVE THE ABILITY TO CHANGE THE SCRIPT OF YOUR LIFE.

— JAZZ THORNTON

HOW ARE YOU FEELING?

LIKE, HOW ARE YOU REALLY FEELING?

Refer to this page when you
need a moment to check in on
how you are *actually* feeling.

SO, LET'S START HERE.

HOW ARE YOU FEELING RIGHT NOW?

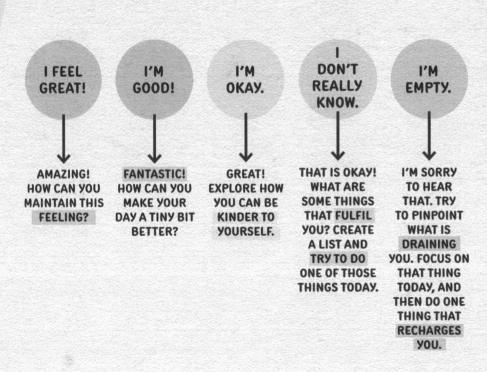

I FEEL GREAT!	I'M GOOD!	I'M OKAY.	I DON'T REALLY KNOW.	I'M EMPTY.
AMAZING! HOW CAN YOU MAINTAIN THIS FEELING?	FANTASTIC! HOW CAN YOU MAKE YOUR DAY A TINY BIT BETTER?	GREAT! EXPLORE HOW YOU CAN BE KINDER TO YOURSELF.	THAT IS OKAY! WHAT ARE SOME THINGS THAT FULFIL YOU? CREATE A LIST AND TRY TO DO ONE OF THOSE THINGS TODAY.	I'M SORRY TO HEAR THAT. TRY TO PINPOINT WHAT IS DRAINING YOU. FOCUS ON THAT THING TODAY, AND THEN DO ONE THING THAT RECHARGES YOU.

TODAY MAY BE TOUGH, BUT TOMORROW

THE SUN WILL RISE AGAIN

Even in your darkest moments there is

hope.

WHAT WOULD MY LIFE LOOK LIKE IF I WAS NOT AFRAID OF ANYTHING?

DON'T GIVE UP.

FEEL-GOOD LIST

Use this space to create a list of things that make you feel good.
These could include your favourite foods, movies, people . . . the
possibilities are endless! Refer to this list in those moments when
you need a reminder of things that can put a smile on your face.

-
-
-
-
-
-
-
-
-
-

MY GOALS FOR THE UPCOMING YEAR ARE...

Use this space to write about some goals you'd like to accomplish this year. Examples: commit to weekly therapy, compliment yourself daily, etc. These do not have to be complicated but we also believe that DREAMING BIG is so great!

SLOW STEPS
EVERY DAY.

BEST COMPLIMENTS I HAVE RECEIVED

Has someone told you that you're a good friend? You're loyal? You're strong? If you struggle to think of any compliments from others, we suggest looking through conversations you've had via text messages, or online. Let us start you off: 'You are incredible for picking up this journal and making it this far.'

YOUR WORDS HAVE THE
ABILITY TO BE PART OF
CHANGING SOMEONE'S WORLD
FOR BETTER OR WORSE.

USE THEM WISELY.

WHAT ARE YOUR BIGGEST INSECURITIES, AND HOW CAN YOU TURN THEM INTO SOMETHING BEAUTIFUL?

'One of my biggest insecurities is that I compare myself to others online and don't think I am good enough. A way of turning this around is . . . what I see online is only a highlight reel, it doesn't paint the full picture. There is only one ME in this world, I am unique and beautiful just the way I am!'

TOP THINGS I LIKE ABOUT MYSELF...

Are you determined? Are you good at art? Can you make people laugh? Use this space to list some things you like about yourself. We suggest staying away from anything appearance-based. Look within and focus on what makes you an AMAZING person.

DISTRACTIONS

Having a list of *helpful* distractions on hand can be a great tool for moments when you are feeling overwhelmed. Have a project you've been meaning to finish? Need to tick things off your to-do list? Loving a TV show at the moment? Write them down and keep them close by for when things get tough.

NOW IT'S YOUR TURN TO CREATE A LIST OF DISTRACTIONS.

You can even go deeper than the example and write more specific things, e.g. which shows on Netflix, friends' phone numbers, what books you could read. The more detailed the better, because when our minds are going a million miles an hour, we need things to be simple.

30 DAYS OF GRATITUDE

Practising gratitude is scientifically proven to make you happier. Use the prompts to help you fill out the table of all the things you are grateful for.

1. ABOUT MY BODY
2. WHAT I FIND BEAUTIFUL
3. A SONG I LOVE
4. AN ACCOMPLISHMENT
5. A FRIEND
6. A SMELL I LOVE
7. SOMETHING THAT MAKES ME SMILE
8. A HAPPY MEMORY
9. SOMETHING I LIKE ABOUT WHERE I LIVE
10. A PERSON CLOSE TO ME
11. A FOOD I LOVE
12. AN ABILITY I HAVE
13. A PERSON
14. SOMETHING I LOOK FORWARD TO
15. A LIFE LESSON
16. A PERSON I LOOK UP TO
17. A PERSONALITY TRAIT I HAVE
18. AN ITEM I USE EVERY DAY
19. MY HOBBIES
20. A HOLIDAY I HAVE BEEN ON
21. A TECHNOLOGY
22. SOMETHING THAT MADE ME LAUGH TODAY
23. SOMETHING NICE
24. A BOOK, MAGAZINE OR PODCAST
25. ANOTHER PERSON
26. SOMETHING IN NATURE
27. A GIFT I HAVE RECEIVED
28. SOMETHING THAT BRINGS ME HOPE
29. A COMPLIMENT I HAVE RECEIVED
30. SOMETHING I AM PASSIONATE ABOUT

YOU CAN DRAW OR WRITE OUT THE THINGS YOU FEEL GRATEFUL FOR!

#1	#2	#3	#4	#5
#6	#7	#8	#9	#10
#11	#12	#13	#14	#15
#16	#17	#18	#19	#20
#21	#22	#23	#24	#25
#26	#27	#28	#29	#30

HOPE IS REAL, CHANGE IS POSSIBLE.

– JAZZ THORNTON

WRITE A PEP TALK TO GIVE YOURSELF THE NEXT TIME YOU FEEL SAD, UPSET OR FULL OF DOUBT.

THINK OF WAYS TO SHOOT DOWN THE NEGATIVE THOUGHTS THAT MAKE YOU FEEL BAD.

WRITE A SHORT LETTER TO YOURSELF ABOUT WHY
GETTING HELP IS A STRENGTH, NOT A WEAKNESS.

Asking for help doesn't make you weak, it makes you smart.

— PAULA FAKALATA, REVOLUTION TOUR

WHO IS ON MY TEAM?

Having a solid support network when fighting mental illness is important. This activity will help you highlight possible people that you can reach out to for help, support and inspiration. It's a good idea to transfer this list to your phone, so that you always have these details on you.

NAME **Frida**
RELATIONSHIP   Best friend
CONTACT   02111111111
frida.grace@internet.com

NAME **Nathan**
RELATIONSHIP   Therapist
CONTACT   022222222
nathan@therapy.com

NAME **Mrs. Jack**
RELATIONSHIP   School Counsellor
CONTACT   Mon-Fri
9.30 am — 3 pm
School

NAME **@VOH**
RELATIONSHIP   Inspiration!
CONTACT   IG: @voicesofhope

NAME **Mr. Lewis**
RELATIONSHIP   Teacher
CONTACT   027777777
mr.lewis@school.com

NAME **Dr. Steph**
RELATIONSHIP   Doctor
CONTACT   0800-DOCTOR
doctor_steph@hospital.com

NOW IT IS YOUR TURN.

Fill in the table and if you struggle to think of people, you can reach out to others for ideas, or write down helplines or even helpful websites or social media accounts that lift you up!

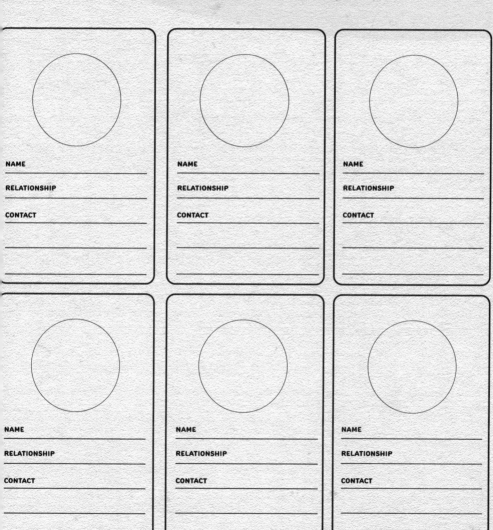

NAME _____

RELATIONSHIP _____

CONTACT _____

_____

_____

NAME _____

RELATIONSHIP _____

CONTACT _____

_____

_____

NAME _____

RELATIONSHIP _____

CONTACT _____

_____

_____

NAME _____

RELATIONSHIP _____

CONTACT _____

_____

_____

NAME _____

RELATIONSHIP _____

CONTACT _____

_____

_____

NAME _____

RELATIONSHIP _____

CONTACT _____

_____

_____

DOTTED NOTE PAGES

Using dotted note pages, rather than the standard ruled, is a great way to get creative. Use a dotted notebook to create your own daily activities, graphs and reminders to keep track of your mental state.

FOR EXAMPLE, I TRACKED MY ANXIETY EVERY DAY LIKE THIS;

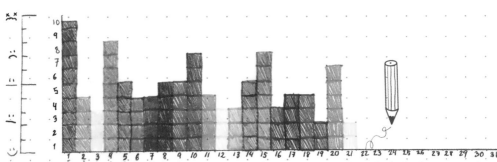

...AND GOT CREATIVE LIKE THIS;

HOLD ON

PEOPLE CAN ONLY HELP YOU WITH WHAT INFORMATION YOU GIVE THEM.

ACT

We can talk about making change — dream about it, think about it — but it is taking action that makes change a reality. When fighting our own battles with mental illness, there came a point where we had to start to put in the hard work and change some of the beliefs, responses and behaviours that were holding us back.

In this section we have compiled activities and tools that we both used during our own fights. Things that will help you start to take small steps towards tangible change. This section won't be easy, but it will be worth it.

Remember it is okay to take your time — go back to the preparation section and read over things like your top 5 songs or quotes. Read them, listen to them, do things that give your mind some peace.

This is your action stage.

WHAT THINGS ARE YOU GOOD AT? BE CREATIVE AND DON'T COMPARE YOURSELF TO OTHERS.

(BONUS POINTS IF YOU CAN NAME 5 THINGS OR MORE!)

YOU ARE WORTH FIGHTING FOR

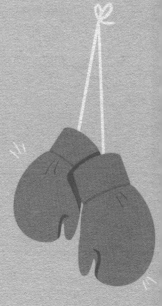

AFFIRMATIONS

WHAT IF WE SPOKE TO OURSELVES AS KINDLY AS WE SPOKE TO OUR FRIENDS?

Positive self-talk and affirmations are proven to increase happiness, so we want to challenge you to create some positive affirmations for moments when you need a boost.

NOW IT IS YOUR TURN!

Use this space to brainstorm some ideas of affirmations that you can transfer onto Post-It notes or cards.

Start each day by reading your affirmations out loud. Remember your mind is always listening to what you say.

SO BE KIND TO YOURSELF!

DO THIS EXERCISE WHEN YOU'RE FEELING GOOD. IF YOU'RE STRUGGLING, ASK SOMEONE SUPPORTIVE TO HELP YOU BRAINSTORM.

I AM FEELING...
I AM THINKING...

It is good to take time to *separate yourself from your feelings* and know what to do when you are feeling a certain way. This exercise can help you dodge any unnecessary worrying when you find yourself in a negative space of mind.

REMEMBER THAT BAD THOUGHTS DO NOT DEFINE YOU, THEY ARE ONLY THOUGHTS, NOT NECESSARILY FACTS.

SOMETIMES I FEEL...	...AND THEN I CAN DO THIS
Useless Like a waste of space	– Ask someone close to me if I can help them with something (errands, cooking, cleaning)
Angry or frustrated	– BREATHE – Meditate
Like I am a burden	– Remember that I am not on an easy journey, and my requirements or demands might be different right now than what people are used to

SOMETIMES I FEEL . . .	. . . AND THEN I CAN DO THIS

ADVANTAGES VS. DISADVANTAGES

Do you feel that your current challenges are giving you comfort, control or even an identity? We hope this activity helps you realise that your illness is not giving you much and that fighting for freedom is so worth it.

To do this activity, on one side write the advantages of staying unwell, and on the other side write the disadvantages. Once you have filled out this chart, talk it through with someone close to you and try and contradict the 'advantages'. The idea of this activity is to help you realise that the things you think are 'advantages' are actually not, and that there is a whole beautiful life out there waiting for you.

'WHEN I WAS UNWELL I HAD MANY MOMENTS OF WONDERING IF RECOVERY WAS WORTH IT. MY ILLNESS BEGAN TO FEEL LIKE IT WAS ALL I HAD, AND SO THIS ACTIVITY REALLY HELPED ME FIGURE OUT WHAT MY CURRENT SITUATION WAS GIVING ME AND WHAT A LIFE FREE OF IT COULD BE LIKE.'

Genevieve

ADVANTAGES	DISADVANTAGES
Control? (Actually, it's giving me a false sense of control)	Missing out on social events
	Don't enjoy waking up each day
	I cry all the time
	Get angry at the people I love
Identity? (Actually, I am more than my illness. I am a great friend, a good daughter, and a hard worker)	Find it hard to be out in public
	Can't relax
	Can't invite friends over
	Find myself staring into space
	Missing out on opportunities

ADVANTAGES	DISADVANTAGES

★ CORE BELIEFS ★

When it comes to battling mental illness, it is important to understand that you are not only fighting the behaviours or responses, but the beliefs that make us do and feel these things. These beliefs differ for each person, but for me personally these beliefs were 'I am unlovable' and 'I am a burden'.

As mentioned in my book, *Stop Surviving, Start Fighting* — this core belief chart was a key component to my fight. On the chart, you write your negative core beliefs on one side and then on the other side you write down everything that people say or do and other evidence that contradicts those beliefs. You can go through encouraging messages that people have sent you or things that they have done that are opposite to what you believe about yourself.

Jazz x

BELIEFS	CONTRADICTIONS
I'm unlovable	'Love you Jazz'
I'm a burden	'I'm so glad you are still here'
	'Please don't give up, we love you'
	'X and X came to see me in the ward today. They took time out of their day to come and see me, not because they had to but because they wanted to.'
	'Please stop listening to your mind and know that we are not better off without you'

78

NOW IT'S YOUR TURN.

Fill out this chart every time you hear, see or receive anything that contradicts your beliefs. Then, when you feel overwhelmed and controlled by these beliefs, pull out this list and remind yourself that your internal reality isn't necessarily the truth.

THERE IS MORE SPACE TO WRITE THESE ON THE NEXT PAGE ⟶

BELIEFS	CONTRADICTIONS

BELIEFS	CONTRADICTIONS

WHAT IS SOMETHING POSITIVE YOU WISH SOMEONE WOULD SAY TO YOU MORE OFTEN?

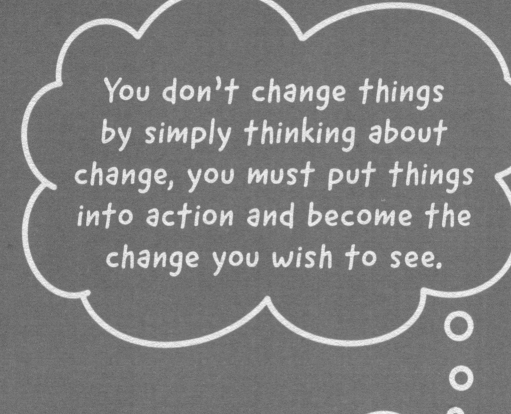

WHAT DO I NEED TO CHANGE IN ORDER TO LIVE THE LIFE I HAVE ALWAYS DREAMED OF?

TO MY YOUNGER SELF

Writing to your younger self can be a great way to reassure yourself that everything will pass. Even if you have gone through difficult events in the past, you are still here and you have survived everything in your life until this moment. Take this space to reflect on how resilient you are, and how much you have overcome.

To my younger self,

I want you to know that things may be tough right now, but you are still here. You are so strong.

You will see parts of the world that you never thought you would, you are going to fall head-over-heels in love, and you are going to finally be happy in your own skin.

Please know that you are worthy, you are loved and that you make other people's lives better by being part of them. Use the support you have around you and be honest with those who are trying to help you. You are so much more than you realise. You light up the room when you walk into it, you make others feel safe and although things may be hard, you wake up each day and continue to fight.

I am so proud of you.

Do not give up.

Love,
Your older self

TO MY YOUNGER SELF...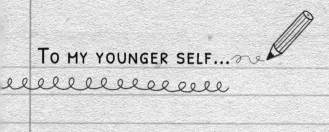

YOU ARE SO MUCH MORE THAN YOUR BODY.

— GENEVIEVE MORA

SELF-CARE ACTIVITIES

Practising self-care is important regardless of whether you're fighting mental illness or not. These activities do not need to be complicated. Things like going for a walk, watching a movie or even having a hot shower can make a big difference.

-
-
-
-
-
-
-
-
-
-

BEST ROUTINES FOR A GREAT START TO THE DAY

Starting the day on a positive note can be achieved in so many ways. Some people start their day by making their bed, as it gives them a sense of accomplishment. Others start their day by reading affirmations to themselves. Use this space to write down some ways in which you can make sure you start your day on the right track.

-
-
-
-
-
-
-
-
-

Tomorrow is a
NEW DAY

SAFETY PLAN

Maintaining safety is important. Professionals often talk about safety plans, as they are a good proactive way to create safety if you enter into a crisis. For each person, this plan looks different. For some, it involves plans to keep you physically safe; for others, it is about avoiding triggers and keeping calm.

TAKE EVERYTHING YOU HAVE PREVIOUSLY DONE IN THIS JOURNAL, FILL OUT THE DIAGRAM AND DEVELOP YOUR OWN PLAN!

WHEN DO I KNOW I NEED TO ACTIVATE MY SAFETY PLAN?	HOW TO FIGHT:	WHO TO CALL:	WHAT I AM FIGHTING FOR:
When my mind starts to spiral into negative thoughts When I start overthinking When I feel like giving up	Distract myself from giving in to urges or behaviours Reach out for help Be honest about what I am going through	Nathan Frida Dr. Steph Helpline	• MYSELF • My family • Future plans • To travel • To be happy! • Help others • Find myself • Pursue my dreams • Confidence

WHEN
DO I KNOW I NEED
TO ACTIVATE MY
SAFETY PLAN?

HOW
TO FIGHT:

WHO
TO CALL:

WHAT
I AM FIGHTING FOR:

REASONS TO RECOVER

Right now it might feel difficult to even imagine a life free of your illness but we are both proof that you can be! We want you to use this space to get creative. Do you want to have a family someday? Travel the world? No reason is too big or too small! There are so many reasons why you should fight for recovery from mental illness.

ENJOY SOCIAL ACTIVITIES

LIVE IN another COUNTRY

NOT FEEL ANXIOUS all the TIME

TRAVEL the WORLD

ENJOY WAKING UP IN THE MORNING

reasons to RECOVER

ENJOY FAMILY gatherings

TO PROVE TO MYSELF THAT I CAN

BE HAPPY!

SPEND quality TIME with friends

GET Married

HAVE a FAMILY

PLAY SPORTS AGAIN

Flip your book this way!

WORRY TREE

Work your way through this graph, answering the questions as you go. This should help you slow down, regroup and lessen the worry you're experiencing right now. Refer to this page any time you notice that you're worrying.

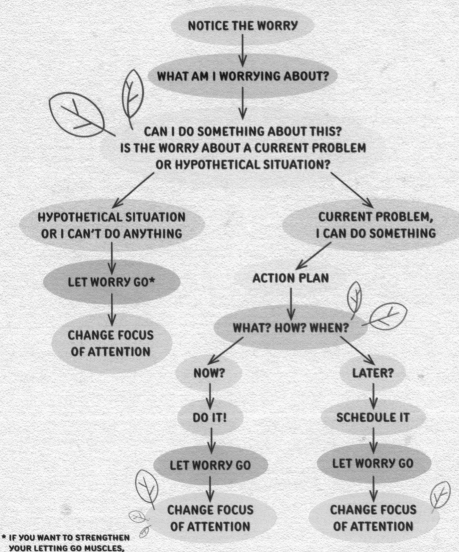

NOTICE THE WORRY

WHAT AM I WORRYING ABOUT?

CAN I DO SOMETHING ABOUT THIS?
IS THE WORRY ABOUT A CURRENT PROBLEM
OR HYPOTHETICAL SITUATION?

HYPOTHETICAL SITUATION
OR I CAN'T DO ANYTHING

CURRENT PROBLEM,
I CAN DO SOMETHING

LET WORRY GO*

ACTION PLAN

CHANGE FOCUS
OF ATTENTION

WHAT? HOW? WHEN?

NOW?

LATER?

DO IT!

SCHEDULE IT

LET WORRY GO

LET WORRY GO

CHANGE FOCUS
OF ATTENTION

CHANGE FOCUS
OF ATTENTION

* IF YOU WANT TO STRENGTHEN
YOUR LETTING GO MUSCLES,
TRY LEARNING MINDFULNESS.

THERE IS A BEAUTIFUL LIFE WAITING FOR YOU.

ANXIETY EXERCISE
5 SENSES

Everyone experiences worries but
sometimes anxiety can be overwhelming.

'Anxiety to me is sweaty palms, butterflies, and fast thoughts.
Anxiety can make you feel like everything is falling apart.
One of the best lessons I ever learned is that anxiety is just
a feeling, it cannot harm you and it is TEMPORARY.' — Gen

In moments of anxiety, there are many things you can
do to try to get yourself through. Learning to sit with that
uncomfortable feeling is important. When you notice your
anxiety is rising, focus on your five senses to help ground you.

Start by practising this activity in the moments you
feel brighter because then you can add it to your
wellness toolbox to use when things get tough.

5	4	3	2	1
THINGS I CAN **SEE**	THINGS I CAN **HEAR**	THINGS I CAN **FEEL**	THINGS I CAN **SMELL**	THINGS I CAN **TASTE**
1. A Poster	1. Birds	1. My cat	1. Cooking	1. Cold water
2. A Lamp	2. The wind	2. My pillow	2. Fresh air	
3. A Plant	3. Traffic	3. My hair		
4. My bag	4. Podcast			
5. My book				

YOU CAN COME BACK TO
THIS PAGE WHENEVER YOU
FEEL LIKE YOU NEED TO
GROUND YOURSELF.

THERE IS MORE SPACE TO WRITE
THESE ON THE NEXT PAGE⟶

1. _____   1. _____   1. _____
2. _____   2. _____   2. _____
3. _____   3. _____   3. _____
4. _____   4. _____   4. _____
5. _____   5. _____   5. _____

1. _____   1. _____   1. _____
2. _____   2. _____   2. _____
3. _____   3. _____   3. _____
4. _____   4. _____   4. _____

1. _____   1. _____   1. _____
2. _____   2. _____   2. _____
3. _____   3. _____   3. _____

1. _____   1. _____   1. _____
2. _____   2. _____   2. _____

1. _____   1. _____   1. _____

1.	1.	1.
2.	2.	2.
3.	3.	3.
4.	4.	4.
5.	5.	5.

1.	1.	1.
2.	2.	2.
3.	3.	3.
4.	4.	4.

1.	1.	1.
2.	2.	2.
3.	3.	3.

1.	1.	1.
2.	2.	2.

1.	1.	1.

YOU MAY HAVE A DIAGNOSIS, BUT YOU ARE NOT YOUR DIAGNOSIS.

Stop looking for happiness in the same place that you lost it.

MY IDEAL DAY WOULD BE...

I AM NOT MY ILLNESS

When faced with a diagnosis or illness, it is easy to feel like your diagnosis defines you. Let us tell you, that is far from the truth. You may have a diagnosis but you are NOT your diagnosis. Your diagnosis may be helpful to inform your understanding and recovery, but you are so much more than a label. Use this activity to write about YOU!.

You can use this activity to help you separate yourself from your illness.

On this page you can write down who YOU are.

NO MENTIONS OF YOUR ILLNESS/ DIAGNOSIS ON THIS PAGE ARE ALLOWED!

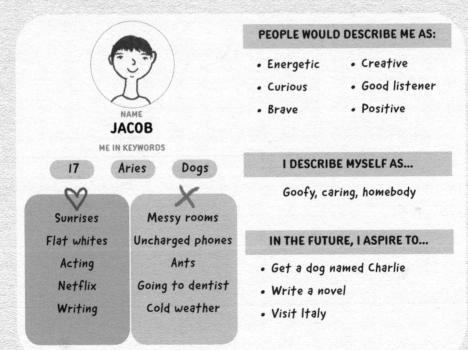

NAME
JACOB

ME IN KEYWORDS

17 · Aries · Dogs

♥
Sunrises
Flat whites
Acting
Netflix
Writing

✗
Messy rooms
Uncharged phones
Ants
Going to dentist
Cold weather

PEOPLE WOULD DESCRIBE ME AS:

- Energetic
- Curious
- Brave
- Creative
- Good listener
- Positive

I DESCRIBE MYSELF AS...

Goofy, caring, homebody

IN THE FUTURE, I ASPIRE TO...

- Get a dog named Charlie
- Write a novel
- Visit Italy

NOW IT'S YOUR TURN.

Fill out this profile for yourself with things that are all YOU, not things that can be traced back to your illness or diagnosis.

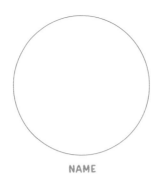

NAME

_____

ME IN KEYWORDS

PEOPLE WOULD DESCRIBE ME AS:

-
-
-

I DESCRIBE MYSELF AS...

IN THE FUTURE, I ASPIRE TO...

-
-
-

MOVE

First of all, well done on completing the action phase. That is a huge accomplishment and one worth celebrating. Action is something that we all need to continue to do throughout our lives, and now you have a few more tools to help you do that.

Now that we have acted, it is time to move forward. One of the definitions of move is to 'change your stance.' In this section we are focusing on how to maintain wellness — looking at dreams, plans and things we can do to continue on our journey.

Now is your time to move.

YOU ARE NOT
A BURDEN

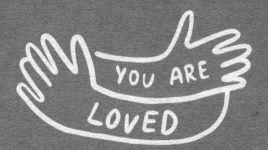

YOU ARE
LOVED

IMPORTANT THINGS
I HAVE LEARNED

This space can be used to highlight important things you have learned from this journal so far or things you have learned throughout your life. Has someone said something wise to you? Did you listen to a TedTalk? Write these ideas here!

UNTIL YOU BELIEVE IN YOURSELF, WE WILL BELIEVE IN YOU.

INSPIRING PEOPLE

Having positive role models and inspiring people to look up to can be incredibly motivating. List some people who inspire you. Think about values and qualities that inspire you, not just achievements.

-
-
-
-
-
-
-
-
-
-

THINGS I SHOULD <u>NOT</u> WORRY ABOUT

We often worry about things we have no control over. It can be helpful to write our worries down, as they can then seem less powerful. List some things you want to stop worrying about, then start working on doing this. *You can use the activity on page 94 to help you through this process.*

Ask yourself,

'Is engaging in these behaviours getting me closer to my goals?'

GOALS & DREAMS

Dreaming and goal-setting can be an amazing tool to help you through moments where you want to give up. Even just pursuing your values can increase your well-being and help you through tough times. When you are faced with an urge or behaviour ask yourself:

'IS ENGAGING IN THIS BEHAVIOUR OR URGE GOING TO GET ME CLOSER TO MY GOALS? IS IT TAKING ME CLOSER TO MY VALUES?'

This page is a place for you to brainstorm your goals and dreams. Put aside 15 minutes and just let your ideas flow.
(You can come back and add more ideas later, too!)

NO IDEA IS A BAD IDEA!

Flip your book this way and get dreaming!

**COME BACK TO THIS PAGE
AS A REMINDER OF <u>WHY</u> YOU
ARE FIGHTING SO HARD.**

THE WORLD IS BETTER WITH YOU IN IT

PLACES I WOULD LOVE TO GO

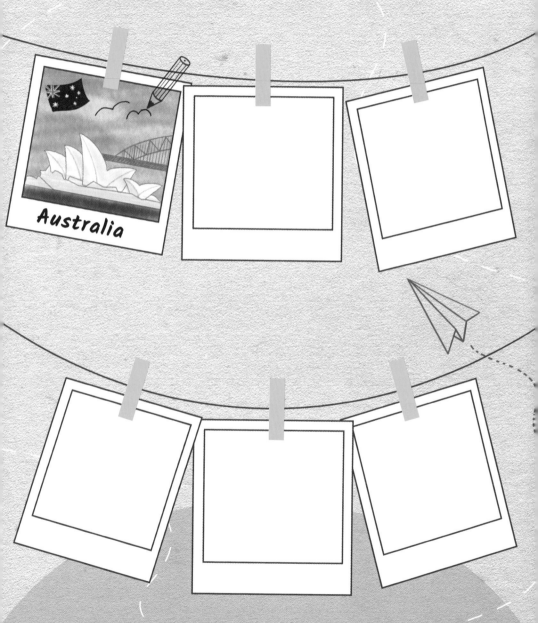

Australia

SCRAPBOOKING

On these pages you can take your time to draw, or put in photos of some memories you cherish. It does not have to be a life-changing moment or time, it can just be something small that you have experienced that you feel lucky that you were a part of.

Our first sleepover!

Seeing each other after lockdown!

NOW IT'S YOUR TURN.

Take a moment to think about some important moments in your life that you want to cherish. You can get creative and draw, or print out photos or pictures that remind you of happy memories.

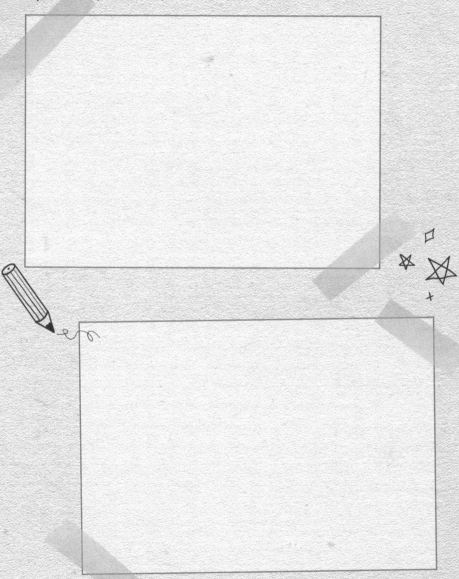

MORE OF THESE ON THE NEXT PAGE ⟶

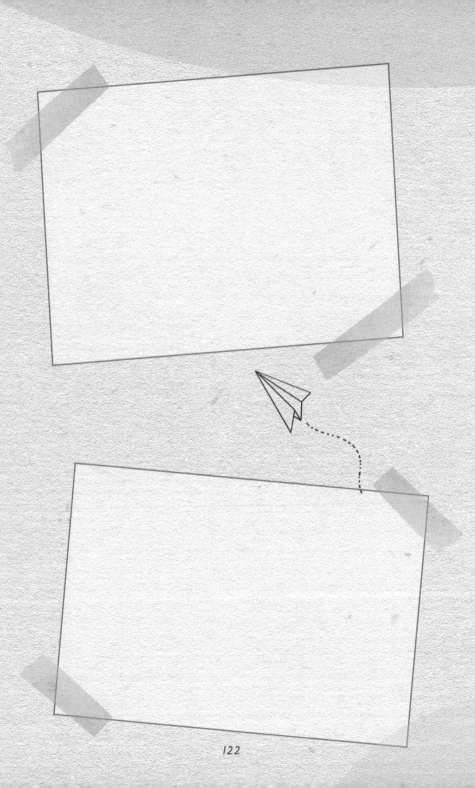

The fact you continue to wake up each day and fight is incredible, and it's something you should be proud of.

LETTER TO MY FUTURE SELF

It is really hard to fight if you don't know what you are fighting for. When I was struggling, I wrote a letter called 'Dear Suicidal Me'. This letter was filled with things about who to call, what I was fighting for and reminding me of why I was fighting. When you are experiencing heightened emotions it can be really hard to remember these things, so I found it really helpful to write them in a letter to myself.

Take your safety plan from page 91 and write a letter to your future self on the next page.

HERE WAS MINE:

Jazz x

Dear Suicidal Me,

If you are reading this, then I am guessing things aren't going too well for you. I know that it probably seems impossible, that you have gone around in another circle and that it would be better with you gone. You think you are a burden to everyone around you and that no one could possibly love you — but you are wrong. There are people who love you. READ the list that you wrote, the list of every single time those closest to you have said 'I love you' or 'I'm proud of you' ...

You ARE loved and you have rock-hard evidence right in front of you. You know what you need to do to bring yourself back up from this space: put on inspirational music (not sad music like you always do, you know this makes you feel worse yet you still choose to do it).

Text Esther, Libby or Wayne — remember, you are not alone and people care, so please get over your pride and fear and reach out. They would rather have you messy and alive than not here at all.

You are so close to being free of this all, don't give up now.

Jazz, you know the process if you attempt to take your life and fail again ... Hospital, mental health wards, tubes down your throat ... Let's not do that again when you can choose right now for that to not be your reality. Remember who and what you are fighting for, people DO care about you and you have a future ... You have gone through this before, many times in fact, and I know this because I am currently writing this letter believing in your future (a day you would have never had if you lost your life last time).

It's not about battling your past but fighting for your future — start fighting right now, take those steps ...

You got this.

All my love, Jazz

DEAR FUTURE SELF...

GOAL ACTIVITY

Usually when we are faced with a bundle of complications, we tend to try to solve everything at once, or try to find one easy way to get to a solution. That mindset can cause a lot of stress and negative thoughts as it seems impossible to get there and is overwhelming.

Instead of seeing your complications as a whole, try to take another look from a different perspective and see each step as an accomplishment. Once you overcome one bump in the road, you are one step closer to your goal.

Use this activity to figure out where you want to go, and how to get there.

#4 WORK ON WHAT NEEDS TO CHANGE

GET BETTER!

#1 GET HELP

#5 PURSUE CHANGE

#3 UNDERSTAND MY NEEDS

#2 OPEN UP TO OTHERS

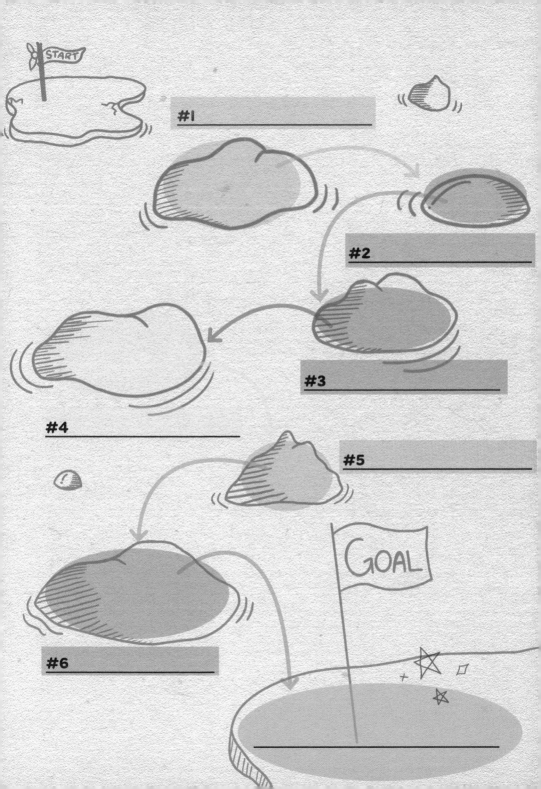

START

#1 _____

#2 _____

#3 _____

#4 _____

#5 _____

#6 _____

GOAL

_____

MY NEXT STEPS

We are so proud of you for making it this far. You are nearly at the end of this journal but your journey to wellness continues. Use this page to plan out what your next steps will be. Do you need to access professional help? Call a friend? Put up the affirmation notes on your mirror? Review the amazing work you've done so far? Having a plan in place for what to do next will help you stay on track.

- [ ] _____
- [ ] _____
- [ ] _____
- [ ] _____
- [ ] _____
- [ ] _____
- [ ] _____
- [ ] _____
- [ ] _____
- [ ] _____

Recovery is possible.
We are proof.

DEAR READER,

WELL DONE FOR MAKING IT TO THE END OF THIS JOURNAL.

WE KNOW AT TIMES IT MAY HAVE BEEN HARD AND CONFRONTING — BUT IT IS OUR HOPE THAT IT HAS EQUIPPED YOU WITH TOOLS, ENCOURAGEMENT AND MOTIVATION TO KEEP ON FIGHTING.
WE KNOW THAT FIGHTING IS NEVER EASY — IN FACT, THE VERY DEFINITION OF FIGHTING IS TO 'ENGAGE IN A BATTLE OR WAR, FIGHT TO OVERCOME AND DESTROY ADVERSITY.' WE KNOW THAT THE FIGHT CAN BE HARD AND EXHAUSTING AT TIMES, WE KNOW THAT IT CAN FEEL LIKE YOU ARE FOREVER IN A LOSING BATTLE, BUT BOTH OF US STAND AS PROOF THAT NO MATTER HOW HARD THE SITUATION YOU CAN GET THROUGH.

TAKE THESE ACTIVITIES AND TOOLS ON THE REST OF YOUR JOURNEY AND USE THEM WHENEVER YOU NEED TO. MAKE SURE YOU CELEBRATE THE MOMENTS OF SUCCESS ALONG THE WAY.

REMEMBER THAT HOPE IS NEVER LOST. YES, SOMETIMES OUR SITUATIONS CAN BLIND US FROM SEEING IT AND WHEN THAT HAPPENS IT BECOMES OUR JOB TO FIGHT TO FIND THAT HOPE ONCE AGAIN.

HOPE IS REAL. CHANGE IS POSSIBLE. WE BELIEVE IN YOU.

Jazz x *Genevieve*

WE'RE ALL REALLY JUST A WORK IN PROGRESS.

MY JOURNEY CONTINUES NOW

HELPLINES

NEW ZEALAND

1737, NEED TO TALK? — Free call or text 1737 from any landline or mobile phone, 24 hours a day 7 days a week.

ANXIETY NEW ZEALAND — 0800 ANXIETY (0800 269 4389)

DEPRESSION HELPLINE — 0800 111 757 or free text 4202 (to talk to a trained counsellor about how you are feeling or to ask any questions) (available 24/7)

HEALTHLINE — 0800 611 116

KIDSLINE — 0800 54 37 54 (0800 KIDSLINE) for young people up to 18 years of age (available 24/7)

LIFELINE — 0800 543 354 (0800 LIFELINE) or free text 4357 (HELP) (available 24/7)

PARENT HELP – 0800 568 856 for parents/whānau seeking support, advice and practical strategies on all parenting concerns. Anonymous, non-judgemental and confidential.

RAINBOW YOUTH — (09) 376 4155 available 11am–5pm weekdays.

RURAL SUPPORT TRUST — 0800 787 254

SAMARITANS — 0800 726 666 (available 24/7)

SHINE (DOMESTIC VIOLENCE) — 0508 744 633 available 9am–11pm, 7 days a week.

SKYLIGHT — 0800 299 100 for support through trauma, loss and grief; 9am–5pm weekdays.

SPARX.ORG.NZ — online e-therapy tool provided by the University of Auckland that helps young people learn skills to deal with feeling down, depressed or stressed.

SUICIDE CRISIS HELPLINE — 0508 828 865 (0508 TAUTOKO) a free, nationwide service available 24 hours a day, 7 days a week and is operated by highly trained and experienced telephone counsellors who have undergone advanced suicide prevention training.

SUPPORTING FAMILIES IN MENTAL ILLNESS — 0800 732 825

THELOWDOWN.CO.NZ — or email team@thelowdown.co.nz or free text 5626

WHAT'S UP — 0800 942 8787 (for 5–18 year olds). Phone counselling is available Monday to Friday, 12 noon–11pm and weekends, 3pm–11pm. Online chat is available from 1pm–10pm Monday to Friday, and 3pm–10pm on weekends.

WOMEN'S REFUGE — 0800 733 843 (0800 REFUGE) for women living with violence, or in fear, in their relationship or family.

WWW.DEPRESSION.ORG.NZ — includes The Journal online help service.

YOUTHLINE — Free call 0800 376 633, Free text 234, talk@youthline.co.nz

INTERNATIONAL

AUSTRALIA
LIFELINE — 13 11 14
KIDSLINE — 1800 55 1800
BEYOND BLUE — 1300 22 4636

USA
SUICIDE PREVENTION HELPLINE — 1 800 273 8255
CRISIS TEXT LINE — text HOME to 741741

UK
1 800 SUICIDE — 1 800 784 2433
1 800 273 TALK — 1 800 273 8255
UK SUICIDE HOTLINE — 08 457 90 90 90
CRISIS TEXT LINE — text 85258

CANADA
CRISIS SUPPORT — 1 833 456 4566
CRISIS TEXT LINE — text HOME to 686868

PENGUIN

UK | USA | Canada | Ireland | Australia
India | New Zealand | South Africa | China

Penguin is an imprint of the Penguin Random House group of companies,
whose addresses can be found at global.penguinrandomhouse.com.

Penguin
Random House
New Zealand

First published by Penguin Random House New Zealand, 2021

3 5 7 9 10 8 6 4

Design and illustrations by Frida Lindström
Author photograph by Maddie Graeme
Prepress by Image Centre Group
Printed and bound in China by Toppan Leefung Printing Limited

A catalogue record for this book is available from the National Library of New Zealand.

ISBN 978-0-14-377567-6

penguin.co.nz

MIX
Paper from
responsible sources
FSC® C104723